MATTHEW P

BIOGRAPHY OF THE HOLL`

MIKE TERRY

TABLE OF CONTENTS

- INTRODUCTION

- CHAPTER ONE

- CHAPTER TWO

- CHAPTER THREE

- CHAPTER FOUR

- CHAPTER FIVE

- CONCLUSION

INTRODUCTION

Matthew Perry is a beloved American actor who has won the hearts of television viewers around the world. He is best known for his iconic role as the popular, sarcastic, and lovable "Chandler Bing" on the NBC sitcom Friends. Throughout his prolific career, Matthew has starred in many sitcoms, plays, and films.

Born and raised in Williamstown, Massachusetts, Matthew showed his aptitude for the arts at an early age. He was the son of two successful actors and soon developed a passion for acting himself. After attending various prestigious schools, Matthew eventually relocated to Los Angeles in order pursue his career.

In 1994, Matthew starred in the role that would make him famous: Chandler Bing in Friends. For 10 seasons, he helped turn the show into one of the most iconic American sitcoms of all time. His character's witty one-liners were often cited as one of the reasons behind the show's immense popularity.

After Friends went off the air in 2004, Matthew went on to star in several other projects. He played a key role in the hit TV-series The West Wing, playing the role of White House Speechwriter "Joe Quincy". Matthew has gone to score various roles in movies and plays over the years. His latest ongoing role is that of "Owen Marshall" in the hit ABC series The Odd Couple.

This book provides an in-depth look at the life and career of Matthew Perry. With an extensive overview of his background, noteworthy achievements, and leading roles, this is the definitive biography of one of TV's most successful actors.

CHAPTER ONE
MATTHEW'S EARLY LIFE

Matthew Perry was born on August 19, 1969 in Williamstown, Massachusetts, to Suzanne and John Bennett Perry. His parents were both landscape architects, and his father owned his own business.

The family moved to Ottawa, Canada, when Matthew was just two years old, and he grew up there until the age of 16.

As a child, Matthew was energetically involved in sports and was involved in many organized sports. He was a very talented baseball player, playing in highly competitive teams and was even in consideration to play baseball in college.

His parents encouraged his extracurricular activities, but unfortunately, tragedy struck when his father passed away at a very young age.

The loss of his father affected Matthew tremendously, and those close to him stated that he suffered greatly for quite some time afterwards.

During his teenage years, Matthew began to take an interest in theatre and the arts, a field that he had not previously explored. He was accepted into an esteemed arts school, and quickly found himself a part of the theatre program.

His passion and enthusiasm for the craft earned him numerous accolades, which eventually resulted in him landing small roles in television shows and films. Upon graduating from high school at the age of 18, he moved to Los Angeles to pursue acting full-time.

Over the next few years, Matthew landed a number of roles in television shows, such as "Growing Pains" and "Beverly Hills, 90210." Yet it was his role as the ever-so-quirky Chandler Bing on the hit show "Friends" that made him a household name. He quickly became an audience favorite, and the show took off to new heights with his performance.

With the success of his show, Matthew was offered many film roles in Hollywood, which he took with gusto. During this time, he was also becoming increasingly involved in humanitarian efforts, often supporting various social causes.

He even formed a foundation called "Friends Across America" which was designed to help impoverished and homeless children in American cities.

In recent years, Matthew is deeply committed to helping friends and family members who are struggling with addiction or any other mental health issues. He has become a vocal advocate for mental health awareness and has spoken openly about his struggles with addiction. The actor is currently in a good place in his life and is endlessly thankful for the support that he has received over the years.

Today, Matthew is an icon of courage, kindness, and resilience, living a life full of hope and promise. He continues to inspire those around him with his brilliance, charisma, and generosity.

He has given back to his community through countless charitable activities and continues to entertain fans through his brilliant artistic endeavors.

Matthew's life serves as an inspiration to us all to never give up, no matter how difficult the situation may be.

Matthew's resilience began long before he became the household name that he is today. Through every step of his journey, he has remained true to himself and has worked hard for his successes. He is an incredible example of the power of believing in oneself and pursuing one's dreams with tenacity and courage.

CHAPTER TWO
MATTHEW'S EDUCATION AND DEVELOPMENT

Matthew Perry had an interesting and lengthy education, both in the classroom and out. He began his formal education in Ottawa, Canada, where he was born. Perry was enrolled in four different schools before the age of 12, moving around between different countries and cities often.

In Ottawa, Matthew attended Ashbury College for elementary and a part of secondary, until the age of 14. As a child he had already taken an avid interest in music and so by the age of 11 was studying the clarinet.

He achieved grades 7 and 8 level in music exams by the age of 13 and was taking part in various youth bands and choirs.

At the age of 14, the family decided to move to Los Angeles. Here, Perry enrolled in The Buckley School, a private prep school, and continued on with his music studies. Matthew soon achieved grade 8 level again and was a member in several ensembles.

While studying in LA, Matthew began to take an interest in the performing arts, including theatre and drama. He attended workshops and enrolled in drama and acting classes with coaches that helped him refine his skills as an actor.

At about this same time, Perry also began to involve himself in local theatre productions.

By the time he graduated high school at the age of 17, Perry had already decided to pursue performing arts and acting as his career. He attended a few universities for a short time, but he soon began to put more energy into auditioning for acting and theatre groupier opportunities.

At the age of 19, Perry earned his first role in a minor television production. This gave him the chance to prove his worth and demonstrate the talent that he had developed through his studies. From there, his career began to take off.

This was followed by many opportunities, including theatre productions, and movies and TV series. He was featured in numerous hits, such as Friends, Studio 60, Battle Creek and The Odd Couple.

As his career expanded, Perry built himself a long lasting legacy, winning several awards and worldwide recognition. Meanwhile, Malhieue continued to take classes and workshops, refining and developing his skills. He began attending acting classes for adults and doing seminars on script analysis.

The extent of Perry's education and development is clear. He developed a wide range of skills that allowed him to become an international superstar.

This is why Matthew Perry's education and development is so impressive: he was able to develop all the necessary skills and knowledge required to become one of Hollywood's most successful stars.

Although his school days may be over, Perry is still a student of the art of acting. He continues to refine his skills and stays abreast of the industry's latest developments. Matthew Perry is a great example of what can be achieved through hard work and dedication.

He has always strived to make sure he is constantly developing and learning, and it is this kind of attitude that allowed him to build the life and career of his dreams.

CHAPTER THREE
MATTHEW'S PERSONAL EXPERIENCE

Matthew Perry has had many interesting and powerful personal experiences throughout his life. From a young age, he had a natural talent for public speaking and used it to hone his communication skills.

As he grew older, he learned that communication was not only the key to success, but also the key to understanding. He firmly believed in the importance of listening to others and respecting their opinions.

At the age of 15, Matthew was elected president of the Hebrew Club at his high school. This was his first leadership role and it had many challenges. He had to learn to delegate tasks among peers, listen to their ideas, and make informed decisions that were best for the team. He also had to find ways to handle delicate subjects such as religion and politics and ensure that everyone was comfortable with the topic of discussion. Through this experience, he learned the value of teamwork, conflict resolution, and compromise.

When he turned 18, he joined a debate team to further hone his communication and problem-solving skills. Matthew took part in several local and national level competitions and this experience enabled him to think on his feet, construct valid arguments, and effectively counter opponents. Debate also helped him to gain confidence and develop his critical thinking skills.

Matthew soon found himself in a unique position when he was appointed as a student ambassador to Norway. This was his first opportunity to represent his country and he was honored to have the opportunity. Here again, his natural talents of communication, problem-solving, and diplomacy provided him with a platform to be heard. He formed strong bonds with different individuals and was exposed to different cultures and ideologies.

His conversations also allowed him to share his ideas and explore different possibilities.

The experiences he gained from his student ambassadorship stay with him to this day and influence his professional and private life.

Matthew's strong beliefs in the value of communication, collaboration, and respect provide him with a strong foundation on which to build and maintain relationships. He sincerely believes that strong relationships are essential to a successful career and personally meaningful life.

Throughout his life, Matthew has seen the power of communication, both written and oral. During his professional career, he has also seen how effective communication can be a powerful tool to achieve success.

He also uses communication for personal growth, sharing his experiences for the benefit of others.

Matthew Perry has seen how communication can bridge divides between individuals and build strong relationships. He strongly believes that communication, problem-solving, and open-mindedness is the key to a successful and meaningful life.

From the Hebrew Club to his student ambassador experience, Matthew Perry's personal experience has had a lasting impact on his life. His personal experience has inspired many around him and will continue to do so in the future.

At first, Matthew Perry was a wide-eyed high school student. Now, he is a man who has seen the power of communication and understands how it can bring people together.

He is an example of how a solid understanding of communication, problem-solving, and collaboration can have a profound impact.

CHAPTER FOUR
MATTHEW'S PROFESSIONAL CAREER

Matthew Perry is an American actor who is best known for his role as Chandler Bing on the popular sitcom Friends. He began his career by appearing in several television commercials.

His first acting break came when he was cast as the underachieving student "Mike O'Donoghue" in the ABC sitcom Second Chance. Despite having limited success with the show, it was enough to get him noticed by the producers of Friends, a show that would catapult him to worldwide fame.

In 1994, Matthew Perry was cast as Chandler Bing in Friends, arguably his best-known role. As part of the show's dynamic cast, with the likes of Jennifer Aniston, Courteney Cox, Lisa Kudrow, Matt Le Blanc, and David Schwimmer, his performance received praise from viewers and critics alike. His portrayal of the sarcastic Chandler was endlessly quoted and inspired a host of pop culture references. The show was a success and ran for 10 seasons, earning Matthew Perry a People's Choice Award for Favorite Male Television Performer in 1995.

Following his success on Friends, Matthew Perry took on other television roles. He starred as John Allen in the ABC drama series Studio 5-B, a role which earned him an Emmy Award nomination. He has also made a number of guest appearances in series like Scrubs, The West Wing, and The Odd Couple.

Matthew Perry's career has also extended to the big screen. His film credits include Fools Rush In (1997) with Salma Hayek, Almost Heroes (1998) with Chris Farley, and 17 Again

(2009) with Zac Efron. In addition to acting, he also wrote the screenplay for three of his movies, including Serving Sara (2002) with Elizabeth Hurley, The Whole Nine Yards (2000) with Bruce Willis, and the critically-acclaimed comedy Numb (2007).

In 2012, Matthew Perry returned to television as the star of the short-lived sitcom Go On. The show's premise revolved around a sport's radio show host (Perry) who enters group therapy after suffering a family tragedy. The show was well-received by critics and audiences alike, and earned Matthew Perry another Emmy Award nomination.

In recent years, Matthew Perry has taken on more serious roles in television. He starred as Ted Kennedy in the HBO movie Game Change (2012), for which he received widespread acclaim. He also appeared in The Good

Wife as a lawyer in a recurring arc that earned him a Critics Choice Award nomination. In 2017, he joined the cast of the Netflix comedy The Odd Couple as the neat freak Oscar Madison.

Matthew Perry is an actor who demonstrates both versatility and longevity in his impressive body of work. With a successful television and film career spanning over three decades, he continues to be one of the most beloved faces in entertainment.

His resilience and longevity in the industry have made him an icon within the entertainment industry and has allowed him to become one of the most recognizable names of the last generation. His success and appeal have proven that sometimes friend-zone jokes and sardonic musings can go a long way.

CHAPTER FIVE
MATTHEW'S CHALLENGES AND TRIUMPHS

Matthew Perry is one of Hollywood's most beloved actors. He has starred in some of the biggest television series of all time, including Friends, The Odd Couple and most recently, Go On. Despite success in his professional life, Matthew Perry's personal life has been much more challenging.

Growing up, Perry was considered a shy child, one who was afraid to take chances and who often felt overlooked. In his late teens, he was diagnosed with depression and he had difficulty finding his place in the world.

In order to cope, Perry developed a dependency on drugs and alcohol, which led to a long-term battle with addiction that nearly cost him his life.

At the age of 21, Perry woke up in a hospital bed after an overdose. He had hit rock bottom and he realized he needed to make a change.

He checked himself into a rehabilitation center and began to get his life back on track. During this time, Perry found the one thing that kept him from giving up completely: comedy.

Humor became Perry's way of channeling his struggles and finding a positive outlet for his pain.
He soon began to perform stand-up comedy as a way of expressing himself and found his true calling.

With the help of his friends, Perry was cast in his first television series, the popular sitcom Friends, alongside Jennifer Aniston, Courteney Cox and the rest of the cast. Perry quickly became an integral part of the show and was widely considered the "heart" of the show.

Perry's fame and celebrity status led to a thriving film career, where he starred in over 50 films, including The Whole Nine Yards, 17 Again and Fools Rush In.

Perry also teamed up with good friend Thomas Lennon to create and star in The Odd Couple and go on to write and produce shows including Mr. Sunshine, and the short-lived Go On.

Despite his success in the entertainment industry, Perry never lost sight of his struggles. He dedicated himself to raising awareness and donations to those struggling with addiction or mental illness.

In 2015, Perry launched the Perry House, a program that provided support to people struggling with addiction. In 2020, Perry opened a health center at his alma mater in Ohio, providing medical care to those in need.

Perry's challenges may have been tough, but they never defeated him. He is a true example of triumph in the face of adversity. Thanks to his hard work and dedication, Perry has achieved incredible success in his career while using his fame to help others.

He proves that no matter how hard the struggle, an individual can overcome any obstacle in life with courage and determination.

Perry never forgot the struggles he experienced during his life and was always looking for ways to make a difference.

Not many people can say they have achieved as much success as Matthew Perry, but more importantly, he is an inspiration to many. His drive and attitude towards life have changed the lives of many people and we are grateful for the impact he has had on the world.

CONCLUSION

In conclusion, Matthew Perry is one of the most beloved and respected actors of his time, and is especially beloved by fans of the hit television show, Friends.

He has embodied a wide range of characters from Chandler Bing to Ben Donovan, and his love and passion for acting has never waned. Matthew Perry's career has taken him to new heights and exposed him to a global fanbase, making him one of today's most recognizable actors.

His career has also enabled him to pave the way for a host of other actors and creators, inspiring those within the entertainment industry and the world at large.

Matthew Perry continues to grow and build a brighter future through his work by helping to change perceptions and beliefs of how people are treated in the world. As a humanitarian, he uses his talent and influence to give back and create meaningful stories which impact the lives of many.

Matthew Perry's legacy has demonstrated that his life and work will live on in the hearts and minds of those he has touched. His words, works and spirit will inspire a generation of our youth to push their boundaries, break through inhibition and dare to dream, no matter what the obstacles may be.

His perseverance and passion for his craft are what has enabled him to become an icon and role model to many in the entertainment industry.

Despite his own personal struggles, Matthew Perry has always managed to stay true to himself and strive for greatness. Matthew Perry's career and life are indeed an invaluable part of our collective memories.

"Life is full of mystery and ambiguity--but also possibilities, new paths and a second chance. And it is up to each of us to find our own way." - Matthew Perry

Printed in Great Britain
by Amazon

30494947R00020